The Spiritual Significance of

Malas

~ and ~

Murtis

Karunamayi
Sri Sri Sri Vijayeswari Devi

Sri Matrudevi Viswashanthi Ashram Trust®
No. 14/5, Ashoknagar, 6th Cross, BSK Ist Stage,
Bangalore - 560 050. INDIA.
www.karunamayi.org

Table of Contents

Introduction 1

Rudraksha Malas 3

Sphatika Malas 11

Lotus Seed Malas 17

Navaratna Malas 25

Tulasi Malas and
　　Wearing Combinations of Malas 33

General Guidelines for Malas 37

Surya Namaskara 40

Sphatika and Suvarna Lakshmi Murtis 48

Summary of Mantras 61

AMMA'S FOREST ASHRAM

Introduction

Introduction

The ancient Vedic seers, or rishis, took birth on the Earth many ages ago in order to educate and elevate all human beings. Through the tremendous meditative power that they generated from thousands of years of austerities, they developed an unmatched intuitive power. With this power, the rishis discovered for themselves the differing subtle qualities of various natural substances, and identified those items that are uniquely beneficial for health and spirituality. Everything in existence has its own particular energy, or vibration, and some items have subtle qualities that help us in various ways. The Vedic rishis investigated the special spiritual properties of all kinds of substances, like metals, colors, trees and plants, different kinds of gems, and so on. Whatever they discovered that was of use, they passed on to mankind many thousands of years ago.

In this booklet, the special properties and uses of rudraksha, lotus seed, tulasi and sphatika malas and murtis are described. Many ancient texts have described in detail the advantages of wearing or using these materials, but this information is not widely available today. Information on how to care for and use malas properly is also presented here so that everyone may derive the greatest physical, mental and spiritual benefit from them.

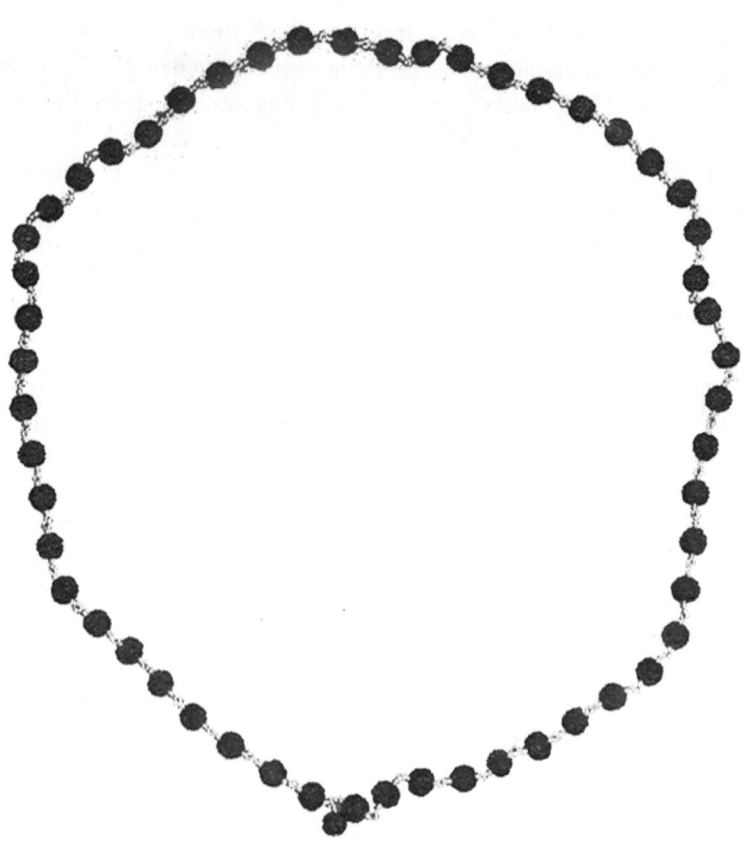

Rudraksha Malas

Rudraksha Malas

Boundless benefits are conferred on those who wear the rudraksha mala with unwavering faith and devotion. Lord Siva is very fond of bilva leaves, vibhuti and rudraksha beads, but it is most beneficial to use or wear these holy items only after understanding their greatness and their proper care and use. According to Sanatana Dharma, those who wear the rudraksha mala are forms of Lord Siva Himself.

Benifits of Wearing or Performing Japa on a Rudraksha Mala

The practice of "japa" involves the repetition of a mantra, using a mala to count the repetitions. One who performs japa with a rudraksha mala will receive the blessings of all sages and all deities.

Wearing a rudraksha mala attracts divine grace to a sadhaka and removes the many hurdles encountered in the spiritual path. Rudraksha beads also have the power to destroy the effects of the most heinous crimes committed out of ignorance and delusion, and they help to purify the karma load.

When we wear a rudraksha mala while performing puja or chanting sacred mantras, all the punya, or subtle energy and merit, will be retained. Without wearing a rudraksha mala, the energy and merit can drain away from our body. Rudraksha beads transmit a subtle spiritual energy to the wearer, and also cause one's energy to rise towards the sahasrara chakra. They also prevent our energy from being drawn down by the gravitational force of the Earth. One should always try to wear at least one rudraksha bead on the body while performing puja, meditating or doing any spiritual practice, but it is actually best to wear a mala of 54 or 108 beads.

It is possible to perform worship of Lord Siva in the form of a rudraksha mala. Worshipping a rudraksha mala with fragrant flowers or bilva leaves while chanting the Siva Panchakshari Mantra will also energize the mala with divine power. By wearing a mala worshipped in this way, one will be blessed with all worldly prosperities and all spiritual desires will be fulfilled.

The devotee who wears a rudraksha mala after bathing and applies vibhuti while remembering Lord Siva by chanting the Siva Panchakshari Mantra, that devotee will shine beautifully with "Brahma tejam," or divine brilliance.

Proper Selection, Use and Care of Rudraksha Malas

Malas containing rudraksha beads that are cracked, broken, or damaged in any other way should not be worn or used for japa. Rudraksha beads that are dried up or that have been eaten by insects are also not good to wear. The rudraksha beads should not be smooth-surfaced, but should have the usual rough, ridged surface.

An old rudraksha mala that has been used for years will not be able to properly absorb the subtle electric vibrations produced by spiritual practices, and should therefore be avoided. Instead, a fresh, new rudraksha mala should be used, as it will have tremendous absorbing power.

There are certain days in the Vedic astrological calendar when it is especially beneficial to wear a rudraksha mala. The day on which the sun moves into a new constellation, or "rasi," is known as a "sankranti." These twelve days are important for wearing rudraksha beads. Most people are aware of Maha Sivaratri, which is the most sacred day of the year for Lord Siva. Maha Sivaratri falls on the fourteenth night of the dark half of the lunar cycle in the month of Magha (February/March). This is the most important day of the year for wearing rudraksha and worshipping Lord Siva. People may not be aware that a minor Sivaratri occurs every month, on the fourteenth night of the dark half of each lunar cycle. These days are also good for wearing rudraksha. In addition, Mondays and the day of the full moon are also good times to wear a rudraksha mala.

It is always advisable to wear a rudraksha mala after sanctifying it by performing mantra japa. One can use the Siva Panchakshari Mantra for this. The mala can then be purified by doing abhisekam with Ganges water (pouring Ganges water over the mala) if it is available. This should be done before wearing the mala, and then once a month or once every six months, so that the mala will remain powerful and energized. When we wear a rudraksha mala frequently, it gives its subtle energy to us and eventually becomes drained; by doing japa and abhisekam to the mala, we re-energize the beads. The merits of eternal worship of Lord Siva can be attained just by wearing the rudraksha mala of 108 or 54 beads that has been energized with japa and abhisekam.

Rudraksha malas can be cleaned at least once a month on the monthly Sivaratri Day or on any Monday. A new brush that will only be used for cleaning the mala should be used. Ganges water is the most auspicious to use, if this is available. Otherwise, any pure water (not obtained from the bathroom) can be used. After bathing, the mala can be worshipped with bilva leaves or flowers and gently rubbed with sandalwood oil. While bathing and worshipping the rudraksha mala, any Siva mantra can be repeated either mentally or out loud.

The rudraksha mala should not be placed randomly; it is important to remember that rudraksha beads are a form of Lord Siva Himself. The mala should never be allowed to touch the floor, as this will cause its energy to completely drain away. It is also considered disrespectful to the divine energy contained in the mala if it is allowed to touch the floor or one's feet.

Rudraksha malas should not be worn while sleeping or while attending to nature's call. Instead, the mala should be removed and placed in a pure, sacred place, like one's altar. Malas should only be worn after bathing, and should be touching the skin. It is good to wear a rudraksha mala throughout the entire day, as long as it is put on after bathing, is removed when answering nature's call, and is removed before sleep.

Rudraksha malas that are worn regularly should not be worn for more than one or two years, as they will have lost their subtle power. After one or two years, the mala can be kept on one's altar or released respectfully into a pure, natural body of water, like a river or lake.

Generally, rudraksha malas can be used for repeating mantras in honor of Lord Siva, like the Siva Panchakshari Mantra or the Mrutyunjaya Mantra. They can also be used with the Gayatri Mantra. The words to these mantras can be found at the end of this booklet.

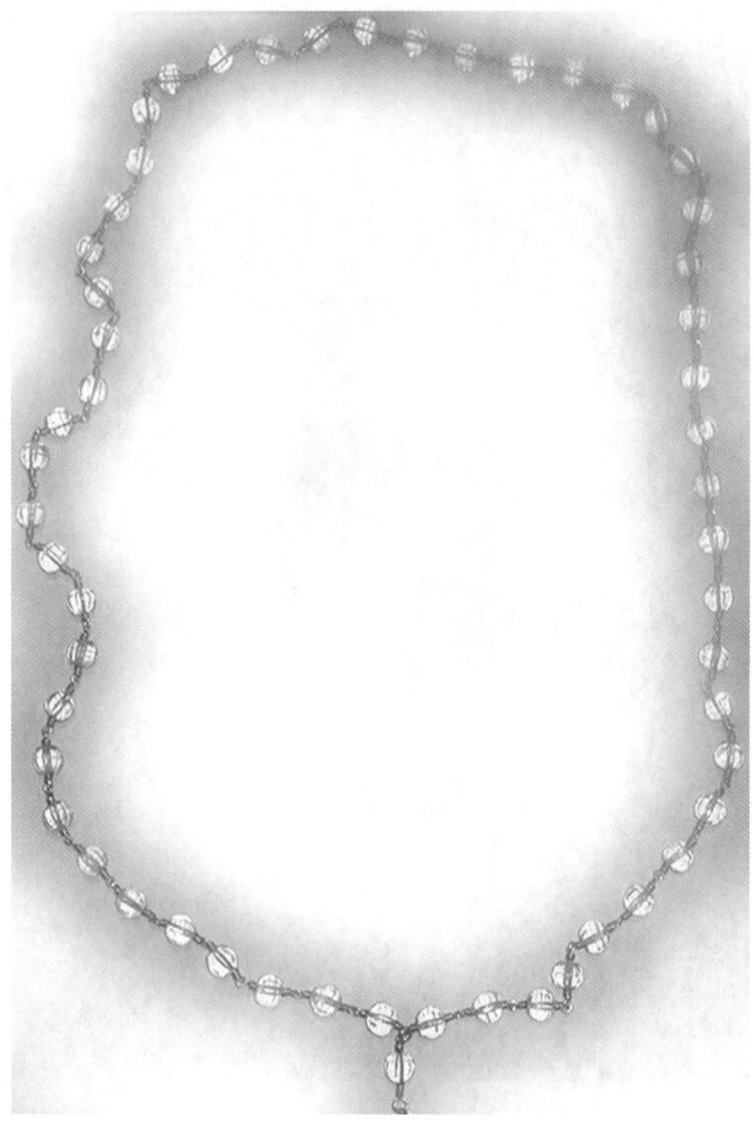

Sphatika Malas

Sphatika Malas

From the Vedic Age until today, those who chant the Vedas generally wear malas of large-sized sphatika beads. The origin of wearing the sphatika mala actually lies in Satyaloka, the celestial abode of Sri Maha Saraswati Devi, for She Herself holds a mala of 54 sphatika beads in Her divine hand.

The 54 crystal beads represent the 54 pure Sanskrit letters or sounds, which are really forms of Saraswati Devi Herself, that were used to create the Universe. Sphatika is therefore symbolic of Saraswati Devi, and contains Her energy. So by wearing sphatika malas or using one for japa, we will be granted Saraswati Devi's own divine qualities.

Benefits of Wearing or Performing Japa on a Sphatika Mala

Those devotees who mentally repeat the Saraswati Mantra 108 times daily with a sphatika mala acquire superb powers of discrimination and purity of heart. Nada Brahmamayi, the holy vibration of highest consciousness, will shine in such a pure heart in the form of a brilliant effulgence. Sri Saraswati Devi will bless those devotees with divine silence, serene patience, an emotionally balanced mind, and atmajnana, or knowledge of the highest Self.

Wearing malas made of sphatika beads guides us toward the spiritual life and benefits us by enriching our knowledge and increasing our compassion and inner strength. All fears and the tendency towards a wavering mind are destroyed, and one's will power is strengthened.

Sphatika absorbs and transmits to the wearer's body all seven colors in sunlight. As each color corresponds to a chakra in the subtle body, the seven colors in the sunlight help all the chakras, or inner lotuses, to bloom beautifully. The heart chakra especially is illuminated by sphatika beads, and eventually one's heart becomes as pure and clear as crystal itself.

Wearing a sphatika mala activates the visuddhi chakra (throat chakra) such that any stammering or stuttering problems will be eliminated and one will have abundant powers of clear, sweet speech.

Sphatika bestows powerful life force on the wearer, strengthens all the 108 spiritual centers in the subtle body, and casts the seven colors of sunlight evenly onto all the chakras. Because diseases are often caused by deficiencies in the seven color energies, wearing a sphatika mala restores our health by supplying the needed color energies. As a result of this subtle strengthening effect, even seemingly hopeless and chronic diseases in the body and mind are destroyed. Even food poisoning can be prevented by wearing sphatika on the body.

Sphatika will not allow one's energy to be drawn away by the Earth's gravitational force, but will encourage one's subtle energy to rise and become concentrated in the sahasrara chakra.

In the worldly life, wearing a sphatika mala increases one's self-confidence and leadership ability, such that one will be honored by society and one's words will be respected.

Proper Selection, Use, and Care of Sphatika Malas

Malas containing beads that are cloudy or not very clear should not be worn. Only clear quartz crystal should be used, and not any other color.

Before wearing the sphatika mala, it is very good to offer it first to a Siva lingam and then to a murti (idol) of Sri Saraswati Devi, or have it blessed by a holy person.

There are certain days that are especially auspicious for wearing sphatika. It is especially good to wear sphatika malas on Tuesdays and Fridays, as both days are very sacred to the Divine Mother. Sunday is also a good day for sphatika, as it is holy to Lord Surya. The day of the full moon is also an extremely auspicious day when Devi rains down divine nectar through the pure rays of the full moon. Wearing sphatika on this day will help to attract and retain this spiritually nourishing lunar energy.

Sphatika malas should not be placed randomly, as they are sacred to Sri Saraswati Devi. The mala should never be allowed to touch the floor, as this will cause its energy to completely drain away. It is also considered disrespectful to the divine energy contained in the mala if it is allowed to touch the floor or one's feet.

Sphatika malas should not be worn while sleeping or while attending to nature's call. Instead, the mala should be removed and kept in a pure, sacred place, like one's altar. Malas should only be worn after bathing, and should be worn touching the skin. It is good to wear a sphatika mala throughout the entire day, as long as it is put on after bathing, is removed when answering nature's call, and is removed before sleep.

Generally, sphatika malas are used during japa for counting repetitions of mantras related to Saraswati Devi or Gayatri Devi, but they can be worn when chanting any Vedic mantras.

Sphatika malas transmit their subtle electric energy to the wearer, and after some time, the beads lose their energy. Malas worn regularly should not be worn for more than one or two years. After one or two years, the mala should be kept on one's altar or released respectfully into a pure, natural body of water, like a river or ocean.

Lotus Seed Malas

Lotus Seed Malas

The holy lotus flower is considered the special abode of Devi, the Divine Mother. All three major forms of the Divine Mother are lovingly described as having eyes, hands and feet resembling the purest, most tender lotus blossom, as being fragrant like the lotus flower, and as bestowing the sacred qualities of the lotus flower on their devotees.

The sacredness of the lotus stems partly from its intimate relationship with the cycle of the sun, which is a powerful source of positive spiritual energy for all people. The lotus flower only blossoms when the sun's rays touch it during the auspicious time of sunrise. When the sun sets, the lotus blossom closes up again until the next morning. Thus, the petals and seeds of the lotus absorb the positive energy of the sun throughout the day and then hold it in overnight. In this way, the lotus seeds become a concentrated repository for solar energy. For these reasons, either wearing a rosary made of lotus seeds or using one while repeating certain mantras can greatly augment one's spiritual energy.

Benefits of Wearing or Performing Japa on a Lotus Seed Mala

When we repeat any Devi mantra or chant the Sri Suktam (a Vedic hymn honoring Lakshmi Devi) while wearing a lotus seed mala, the radiant solar energy is attracted to our body, and we will glow intensely with that divine energy. All sorrows will be dispelled and a divine peace will dawn in our mind. From wearing a lotus seed mala, excellent mental concentration can be obtained, and the face and eyes begin to glow with the radiant purity of the lotus flower itself. For the person who wears the lotus seed mala, even the enemies become friends.

When we repeat mantras while holding a lotus seed mala in our hand and wearing another lotus seed mala around the neck, all the chakras, or energy centers, in the body become activated and begin to blossom. The Divine Mother, in the form of the sacred kundalini energy, touches and cleanses all the chakras. Chanting a mantra once while holding or wearing a lotus seed mala gives the benefit of chanting that mantra one million times without a lotus seed mala. This is the power of the lotus seed mala!

It is especially beneficial to wear or use lotus seed malas on Friday mornings, as Friday is sacred to Devi.

Benefits of Using Either Pink or White Lotus Seed Malas

Lotus seed malas can be made from seeds taken from pink or white lotuses. Although the malas will have the same appearance, the significance of these two types of malas is different.

Special Effects of the Pink Lotus Seed Mala

The pink lotus is the special abode for Lakshmi Devi, the Divine Mother who graces devotees with both spiritual and material abundance. Mother Lakshmi's entire body is described as resembling a beautiful, golden lotus.

If anyone is having financial troubles, there is a very powerful practice that can be performed to alleviate this problem. When a devotee chants the Sri Suktam 16 times a day for 120 straight days while wearing a pink lotus seed mala, Lakshmi Devi is immensely pleased and graces the devotee with abundant wealth and spiritual treasures. Not only will the devotee benefit from this practice, but many generations of the devotee's descendants will also benefit from Lakshmi Devi's beneficent grace.

When any mantra in honor of Lakshmi Devi is chanted with the pink lotus mala either 1000, 300 or 108 times a day, all kinds of poverty are destroyed. All financial problems will be solved. It is not just the material poverty that is destroyed, however. All kinds of spiritual poverty, like poverty of devotion, poverty of truthfulness, or poverty of sweet speech, will be destroyed by the pink lotus mala. The pink lotus mala has a particularly powerful effect on the heart chakra, which is related to devotion and divine love.

Special Effects of the White Lotus Seed Mala

The white lotus is the special abode of Saraswati Devi, and therefore white lotus seed malas are especially sacred to Her. Through the use of the white lotus seed mala, the pure knowledge of the Divine Self is obtained, memory power is greatly improved, and the divine grace of Mother Saraswati is obtained.

When the Saraswati Mantra is chanted 1000, 300 or 108 times a day while wearing or holding the white lotus mala, one's creative abilities are enhanced, and even one's vocabulary is improved. One's speech will become pure and sweet and one's mind will be stable, tranquil and full of divine peace. The mind will become powerful and discrimination will be increased. Supreme wisdom will dawn in the mind of such a devotee.

When the Saraswati Mantra is chanted five million times with white lotus seeds, the Divine mother grants one a profound knowledge of the Vedas, and ultimately the highest Self-Realization is achieved.

It is also very beneficial to use the white lotus mala when chanting the Gayatri Mantra. When this mantra is repeated 1000, 300 or 108 times a day with the white lotus seed mala, many great spiritual benefits are obtained and even the most terrible of sins are completely burned away.

Proper Care and Use of Lotus Seed Malas

Lotus seeds are covered with a very thin, delicate, shell-like layer. Even a drop of water can cause this thin film to rupture, and the seed will lose its energy. The lotus seed mala selected should have smooth, unbroken seeds. Great care should be taken to avoid getting the seeds wet. If the mala becomes dusty, the seeds can be rubbed gently with a clean, dry cloth that has a bit of ghee (clarified butter) on it. The mala should never be allowed to touch the ground or one's feet, otherwise its energy will drain away and be lost.

Generally, lotus seed malas from any color lotuses are used with any mantras or Vedic hymns related to any form of the Divine Mother.

Lotus seed malas should only be worn after bathing, and should be worn touching the skin. In contrast to rudraksha or sphatika malas, lotus seed malas *should not* be worn throughout the day; they should only be worn while doing spiritual practices, when visiting a temple or place of worship, or while attending a homa or puja. It is best not to wear the lotus seed mala while performing worldly duties. The mala should especially not be worn while attending to nature's call or while sleeping. When not worn, the mala should be kept carefully in a box in a pure place, like one's altar.

Navaratna Malas

Navaratna Malas

It is a general Vedic principle that what is found in the cosmos or the heavens, is also found on Earth and within the human being. According to Vedic Astrology, the nine planetary bodies are present in subtle form in our own bodies. We all have a subtle body that is composed of our karma from the many thousands of lives we have lived. This is known as our karma load, and this is what creates the circumstances and events of our lives so that we can experience the fruits of our karma.

Each of the nine planets emanates a particular vibration of energy that has a specific kind of effect on our lives. As the planets rotate and move through the sky in relation to the Earth, they activate different aspects of our karma load by changing the flow of energy in our subtle bodies. This is how the planets perform their divinely appointed work of encouraging spiritual evolution. It is not that the planets "make" things happen to us. The planets simply bring different aspects of our karma load to the surface at different times and cause those aspects to be expressed in the physical world.

We experience these effects in a seemingly negative way as illnesses, mental disturbances, accidents, loss of loved ones, and so on. We are also positively affected by the planetary energies according to our good karma, as well as astrological conjunctions of beneficial energies that occur on holy days.

The Vedas have provided many ways of working with planetary energies in order to reduce the severity of the fruits of our negative karma, and increase our positive connection with the planets. The simplest way to reduce negative planetary effects is to wear a "navaratna mala," which is a necklace or mala composed of nine different stones that correspond to each of the nine planets.

Each planet has two or three precious or semi-precious gems that vibrate according to its specific frequency. When a person wears a navaratna mala, the nine different stones produce an energy field that fills his or her aura and modifies the effects of any planetary energies that fall on that person's body. The presence of the stones will reduce the effects of negative karmas and at the same time enhance the positive karmas.

The Nine Planetary Bodies of Vedic Astrology

The nine planetary bodies of Vedic Astrology are the Sun, Moon, Jupiter, Mercury, Venus, Saturn, Mars, Rahu and Ketu; some of the general problems, blessings and diseases associated with these have been listed below.

The Sun *(ruby or garnet).* Issues related to the sun include lack of willpower and energy. Solar energy brings spiritual luster, physical vitality, and mental cheerfulness. Diseases of the blood are related to the sun.

Jupiter *(yellow sapphire, yellow topaz or citrine).* Jupiter rules over success in life and one's career, honor, and one's progeny. Jupiter bestows piety, nobility, truthfulness, optimism, and a good relationship with one's children as well as one's guru. Diseases of the liver and fat are related to Jupiter.

Saturn *(blue sapphire, amethyst, or star of India).* Saturn is a powerful taskmaster who brings some very difficult karma to the forefront of one's life, and yet some of the most powerful spiritual lessons are learned as a result of these difficult experiences. Saturn brings integrity, wisdom, steadfastness, patience, honesty, love of justice and awareness of right and wrong, true detachment and asceticism. Propitiating Saturn helps to remove difficult obstacles, sorrow, dejection, fear of death, and lack of discipline. Diseases related to Saturn include mental disturbances related to fear and depression.

Mars *(coral, carnelian or red agate).* Mars rules over courage, self-confidence, true leadership, mental and physical vigor. Mars helps us to overcome violent tendencies, anger, insensitivity, impulsiveness, and a cruel nature. Diseases governed by Mars include diseases of the blood and bile.

Venus *(diamond, white sapphire or quartz crystal).* Venus makes us appreciate the beauty and sweetness in life and helps us to have harmonious relations with our spouse. Artistic pursuits are encouraged by Venus, who helps us to overcome a tendency towards sensory overindulgence. Diseases of the reproductive organs are related to Venus.

Mercury *(emerald, green tourmaline or jade).* Mercury rules intelligence, both verbal and written communication skills, sense of humor, and travel or movement. Nervousness, insecurity and anxiety can be overcome with the help of Mercury. Diseases of the lungs, nervous system and intestines are affected by Mercury.

The Moon *(pearl, moonstone or white agate).* The moon rules over one's sense of purpose, the emotions, intuitive intelligence, and love of the fine arts. Honoring the moon gives us a calm, pure mind and helps us to overcome emotional instability, excessive emotional sensitivity. Diseases related to the moon include menstrual disorders and female sterility.

Rahu *(hessonite—a type of garnet).* Rahu governs lethargy and sluggishness, insatiable desires, love of money, power and fame, and general negativity. Rahu is related to such terrible afflictions as drug addiction, suicidal tendencies, and psychic or ghostly possession. Rahu helps to remove our fear and give insight.

Ketu *(cat's eye or tiger's eye).* Ketu rules over obssessive and compulsive behavior, physical accidents, imprisonment, nightmares and involvement in conspiracies. Diseases related to Ketu include diseases of the joints and nerves.

The Use and Care of Navaratna Malas

It is good to wash a new navaratna mala with Ganges water if it is available. One can offer incense to the mala, with an inner attitude of devotion and gratitude for the planets' untiring efforts to help us resolve our karmic bonds efficiently. If a navaratna mala has already been energized by the sacred vibrations of a homa ceremony, it is not necessary to perform any purifications.

Generally, the navaratna mala is worn, and is not used for japa. Every day is a good day to wear this mala, and it is beneficial to wear the navaratna mala as much as possible in order to maintain the positive effects in one's aura at all times. One can take it off at night, however, and place it in a clean, pure place.

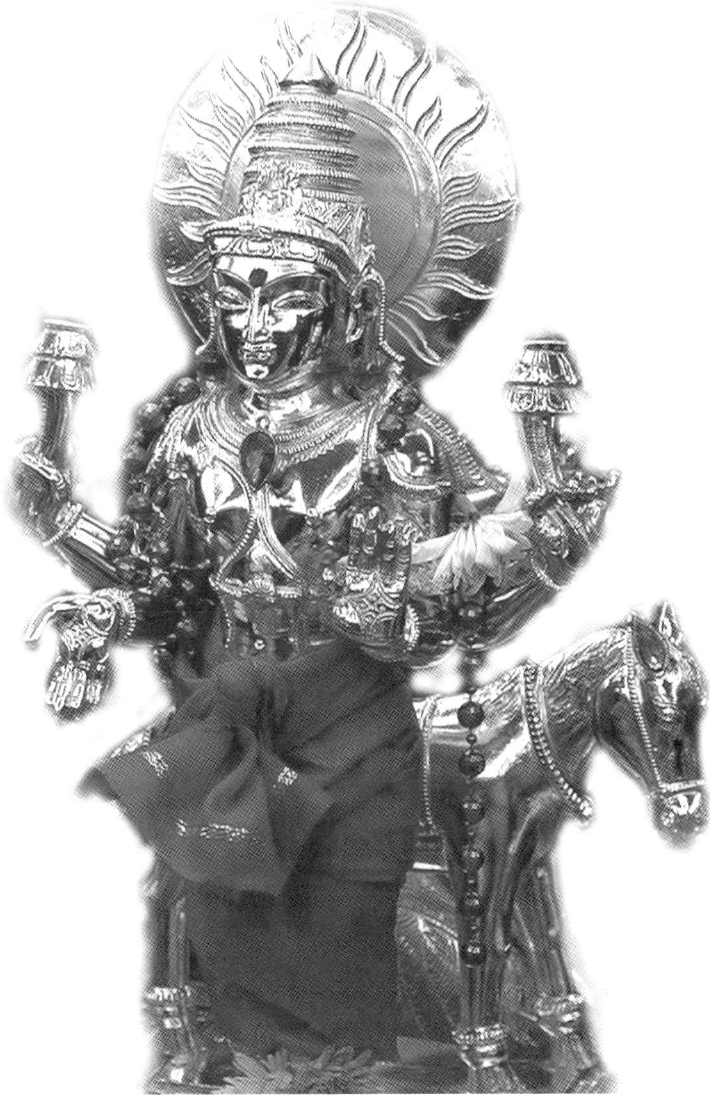

32

Tulasi Malas & Wearing Combinations of Malas

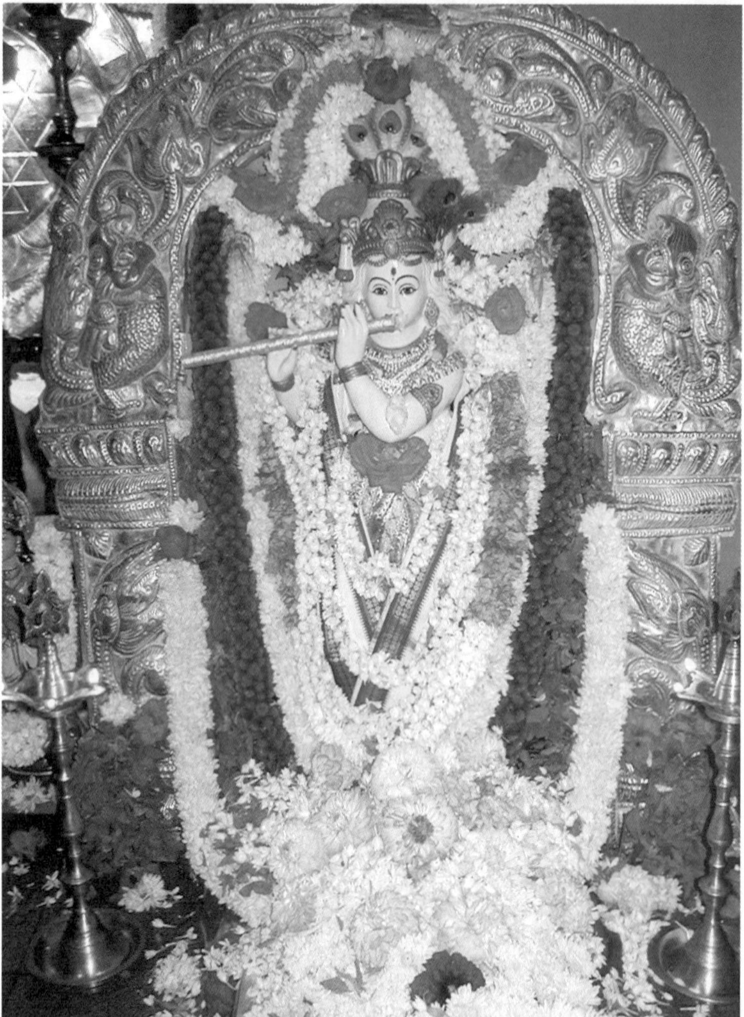

Tulasi Malas

The holy tulasi plant is sacred to Lord Vishnu and His incarnations, like Sri Ram and Sri Krishna. Wearing a tulasi mala enhances devotion, inner peace, purity, and other virtues. Tulasi malas also increase one's knowledge of the true, divine Self, and help to heal all kinds of diseases. It is good to wear a tulasi mala on Saturdays. The same kinds of guidelines (wear only after bathing, replace after one to two years, etc.) apply to tulasi malas as have been explained for rudraksha and sphatika malas. Tulasi malas are generally used for any spiritual activity related to Lord Vishnu or any of His incarnations.

Effects of Different Combinations of Malas

Wearing both rudraksha and sphatika malas together wards off the evil effects of the stars and planets and fulfills all noble wishes. Wearing rudraksha, sphatika and tulasi all together is very powerful and brings success in all one's efforts.

*Wearing a mala while performing or
attending sacred ceremonies is very beneficial.*

General Guidelines for Wearing or Performing Japa with a Mala

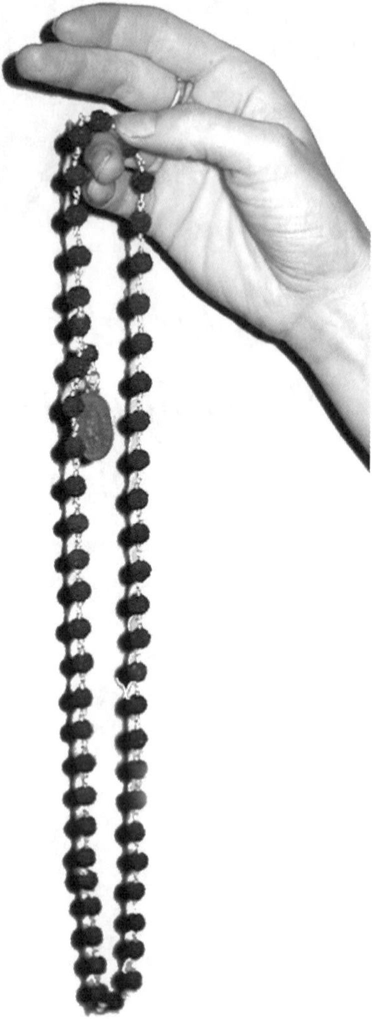

General Guidelines for Wearing or Performing Japa with a Mala

These guidelines have been given so that the purity and elevated spiritual energy of one's mala may be maintained; they are not meant to be overwhelming. The energy in one's mala is absorbed into the subtle body when worn or used for japa; thus it is for our own benefit to keep the mala as pure as possible.

The mala that is used for counting repetitions of a mantra should not be worn on the body; it should be used for one's daily japa only. On the other hand, the mala that is worn on the body can be re-energized by doing japa on it every so often. Malas should never be allowed to touch the floor or one's feet, and ideally they should be touched only after bathing. It is also important not to wear malas while sleeping or attending to nature's call.

A mala should contain either 54 or 108 beads, with an additional bead sticking out from the main loop. This extra bead is known as the "meru bead," and it should be present. The mala should not have 53 beads, with an extra meru bead. It should have 54 on the main loop, with the meru bead as the 55th bead. Or, it should have 108 beads on the main loop, with the meru bead as the 109th bead. In the human body there are 108 main subtle energy centers, and in the brain there are 108 main "jnana kendras," or centers of higher knowledge. Therefore, when we perform mantra japa 108 times on a mala that has 108 or 54 beads, we energize all the 108 subtle centers and the 108 jnana kendras. We can derive the same effect by wearing malas of 108 or 54 beads that have been energized by japa or puja, or the blessing of a holy person.

There is a specific way of handling the mala when performing japa which holds much significance for the energy that is generated. The mala should be held in the right hand, and it should be draped over the ring finger (and the fifth as well). The thumb should be used to move each bead over the ring finger as each repetition of a mantra is completed. The index and middle fingers should not touch the mala during japa. Each finger contains a certain quality of energy, and the energy of the index finger especially is not good for spiritual activities of any kind. In fact, the index finger should not be used for making offerings, for applying kumkum or vibhuti, or even for pointing at anything. One should always use the ring finger or thumb for making offerings, applying kumkum, or performing japa. This is because the ring finger of the right hand contains a nectarean energy that is most conducive to our spiritual evolution, and the nadi, or subtle spiritual nerve, in it goes straight to the heart.

The meru bead is significant because it lets us know when we have completed a certain number of repetitions of the mantra. When we have repeated a mantra 54 or 108 times and we come around to the meru bead, it is very important not to cross over the meru bead if we are going to continue doing japa. Instead, we should turn the mala around so that the last bead we just touched becomes the first bead counted for the next round of japa. That is, bead number 108 (or 54) of one round of japa becomes bead number 1 for the next round.

If we do not turn the mala around and we cross the meru bead, the energy generated from our japa will be rajasic or even tamasic. This kind of japa is known as "rakshasic" japa, because in ancient times demons used to do japa in this way for negative purposes. If we always turn the mala around as we complete each round of japa, we will generate visuddha sattvic qualities—the purest spiritual qualities.

In general, do not allow anyone else to use your mala, or even touch it. Ideally, no one would ever even see one's mala, especially when doing japa. While doing japa, one can hold the mala under a piece of clothing or shawl, or keep it in a bag large enough to put one's hand into. Traditionally, malas are kept inside a cotton or silk bag that has never been used for any other purpose, and they are not taken out. When it is time to do japa, the thumb, ring finger and pinky are inserted into the bag, with the index and middle fingers kept outside of the bag. The beads are then moved with the mala completely inside the bag. If someone sees one's mala while japa is done, the energy contained in the mala will be drawn to them and will be lost; this is why one keeps the mala hidden.

Do not keep the mala that you wear or use for japa on a murti or picture of God. If it is not kept in a bag, it can be placed on the altar itself.

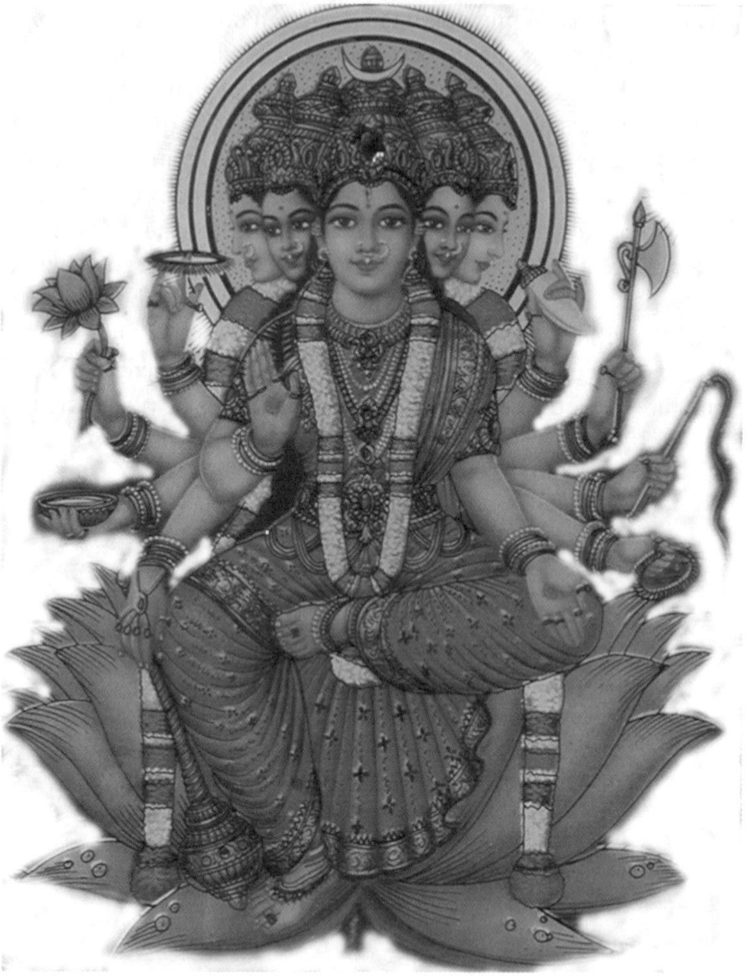

The Sacred Practice of Suryanamaskara

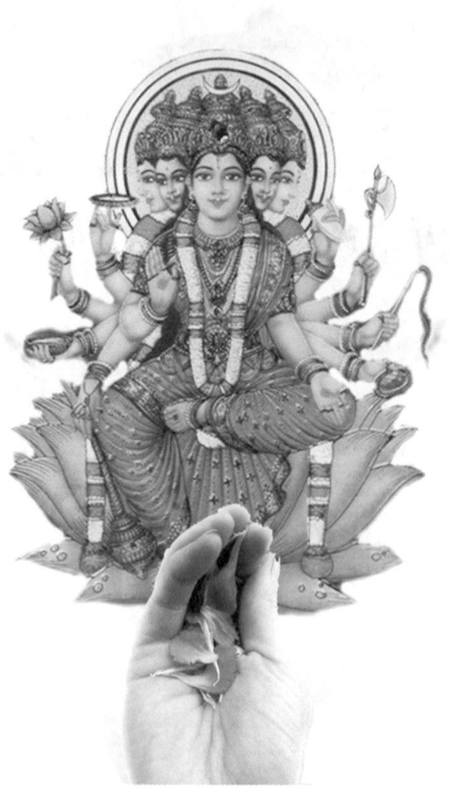

The Sacred Practice of Suryanamaskara

The goal of India's ancient rishis was to impart a sacred culture to mankind that would allow people to live their lives in harmony with Nature, while achieving maximum physical, mental and spiritual strength. It is only when the body and mind are strong that we can live a peaceful life and sit properly for meditation, japa or puja. If our path is selfless service, we also need mental and physical vigor to withstand the demands of working in the world.

One of the most important practices taught by the Vedic sages is the practice of "suryanamaskara." In this practice, we are essentially "plugging in" to the vast storehouse of divine energy that is radiated every day by the sun. The sun is a divine flame lighting up the sky for all creatures on the Earth. All forms of darkness are dispelled by the powerful light of the sun, and the sun's radiant energy is the primary source of life for all creatures, including humans, animals and plants. On a subtle level as well, the sun radiates a powerful spiritual energy that sustains all living beings in the world. This energy falls on everyone equally, but by following the practices advised by the Vedic sages, we can attract the sun's potent energy and absorb it like a sponge. The most important time to absorb the sun's energy is during sunrise. At this time, the light emitted by the sun is extremely auspicious for health and spirituality.

Benefits of Performing Suryanamaskara

The practice of suryanamaskara gives us the energy to carry out all the daily activities and duties with energy and cheerfulness; it also gives us a strong connection to dharma by linking us with the natural cycles provided by Mother Nature for our own well-being. One who does this practice on a regular basis will be firm and steadfast in their spiritual life. Suryanamaskara connects us with the visuddha sattvic energy pervading the atmosphere during early morning, and insulates us from any negative influences we may encounter during the day. Rising early protects us from the negative effects of Saturn or any other difficult astrological energies.

The effects of suryanamaskara are heightened and magnified when we wear rudraksha, sphatika or lotus seed malas. If suryanamaskara is done while wearing a rudraksha mala, one's very life will become radiant with the brilliance of the sun. One will be protected from physical accidents and mishaps. All physical and mental ailments, like high blood pressure and blood sugar, tuberculosis, mental depression and anxiety, and heart problems, will flee from the body and mind like darkness scattered by a bright light. When a sphatika mala is worn while performing the practice of suryanamaskara, the beads absorb the seven colors present in the sunlight and activate all 72,000 nadis in the subtle body. The mind and heart become purified until they are as clear as crystal. Wearing the lotus seed mala will bring divine radiance and tremendous peace to one's heart. One's face will glow beautifully with inner joy.

How to Perform Suryanamaskara

In the practice of suryanamaskara, we are greeting and honoring the Divine Mother in the form of the rising sun, so it is beneficial to imagine Gayatri Devi, the Mother of all the Vedas, as residing within the disc of the sun. Suryanamaskara should only be done at the time of sunrise. First, it is necessary to wake up from bed and bathe, including washing the hair, before sunrise. Wearing fresh, clean clothes, take some pure water (not from the bathroom) and red-colored flower petals, and go outside. The flower petals can be golden, orange, red or bright pink.

It is best not to wear shoes, so that you will be connected with the energy of Mother Earth. Facing east, try to stand in a place where you can see the newly risen sun. Take some petals in your right hand and with the left, pour some water into the cupped right hand. While holding the right hand out in the direction of the sun, chant the Gayatri Mantra out loud. Try not to let the water leak out of your hand while you are chanting the mantra. At the end of the mantra, offer the water and petals to God by gently pouring the contents of your hand onto the ground in front of you. This process of taking petals and water in your right hand, chanting the Gayatri Mantra, and offering the petals in front of you should be done three times.

After doing three repetitions of the Gayatri Mantra, you can also chant the Mrutyunjaya Mantra three times in the same way. After that, you can chant the Saraswati Mantra five times while offering the water and petals. If you run out of petals, just use the water. If you run out of water, you can just chant the mantras while standing with the palms of your hands joined together at the heart, in the traditional Indian gesture of greeting. According to the time available, you can then chant any Vedic hymns you may know, like the Sri Suktam or Purusha Suktam.

Amma has explained the reasons why the Vedic sages developed this practice in the way that they did, as no part of it is arbitrary. The golden or red-colored petals contain a certain vibration due to their color, and this vibration matches the golden-red color of the rising sun. Because of this vibrational resonance, the colored petals help to attract the divine energy of the sun to the person holding them. Water is held in the hand to increase the transfer of the solar energy to the body. Just as water conducts electricity, water also conducts and transfers subtle energy, or prana. This is why it is used in so many Hindu ceremonies. There is a nadi, or subtle energy conduit, in the right hand that goes directly to the heart, and this is why only the right hand is used in this practice.

As you hold the reddish petals and water in your right hand and chant the Gayatri Mantra in front of the rising sun, you are creating a direct connection between the sun and your heart. As the divine solar energy pours into your heart, it will be spread to the rest of the body through the blood as well as the nadi system. Wearing a rudraksha, sphatika or lotus seed mala while performing this practice will greatly enhance the effects by retaining and magnifying the power of the sun and preventing it from draining away.

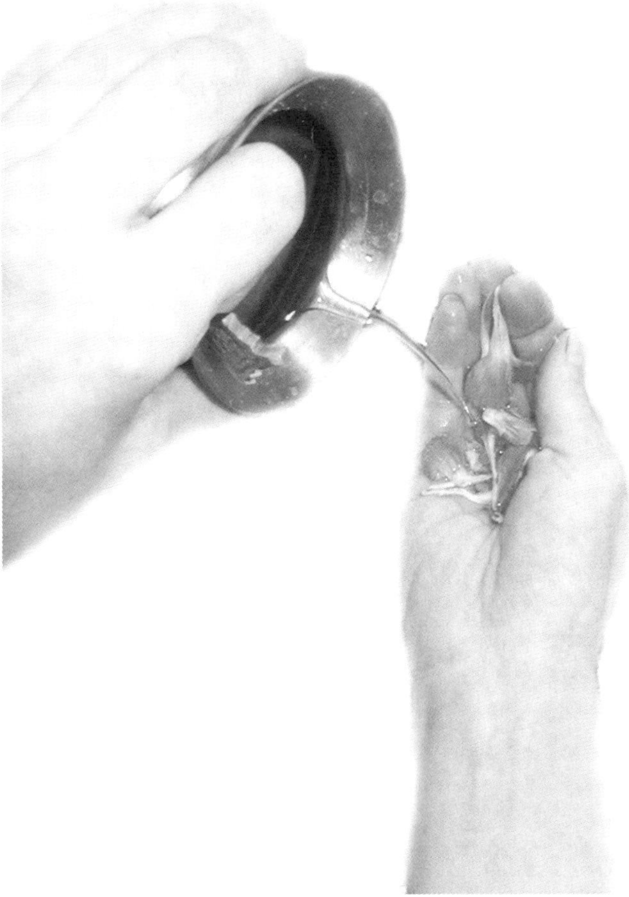

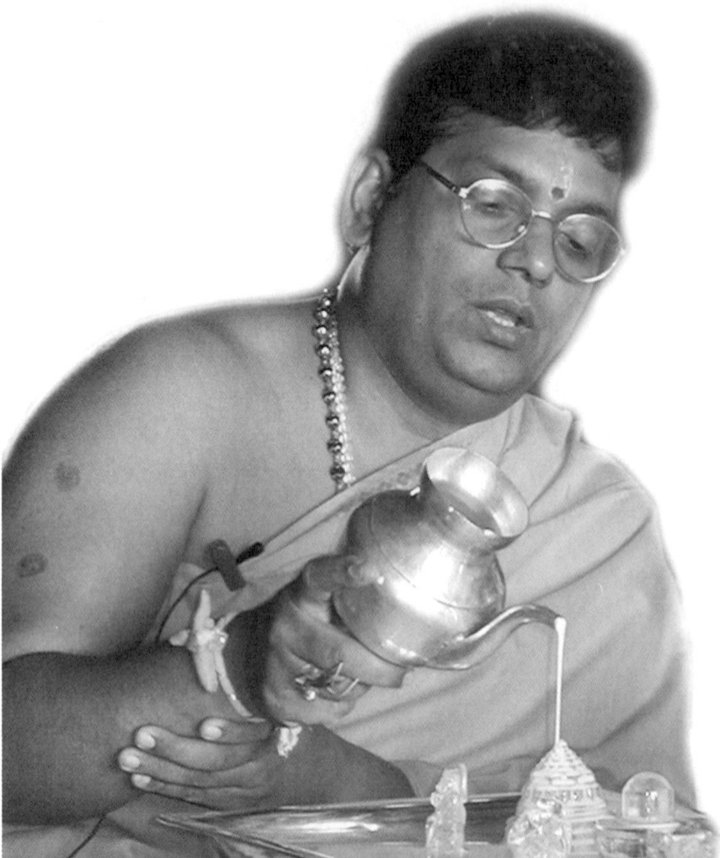

Sphatika & Suvarna Lakshmi Murtis

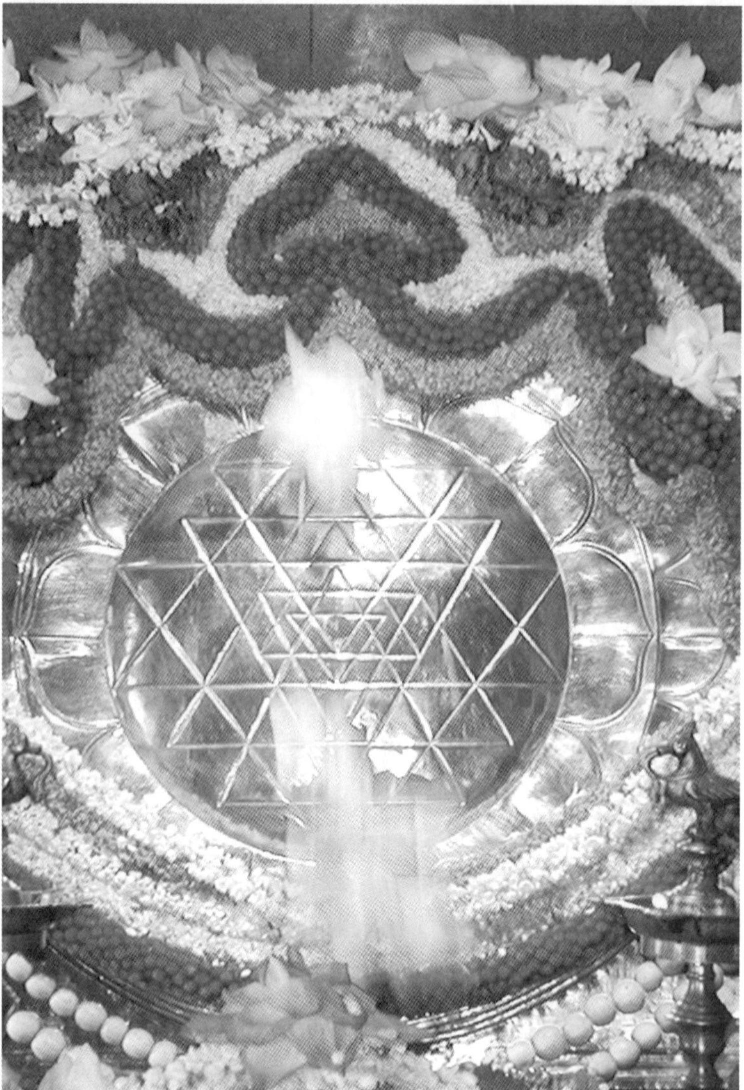

Crystal Murtis

Murtis, or idols, that have been carved from pure, clear quartz crystal that does not have cracks in it are extremely powerful and transmit a wonderful spiritual energy to the one who owns or worships them. It is the karmic opportunity of lifetimes to be able to own or worship a crystal murti of any kind. This is really the result of one's merit accumulated from thousands of births. This section discusses the significance of three types of murtis made from sphatika.

The Greatness of the Sri Chakra

The Sri Chakra, also known as the Sri Yantra, is a pattern of interlocking triangles surrounded by a circular lotus design. This pattern is the most powerful of all yantric designs, and it contains the energy of Sri Lalita Parameswari, the Supreme Divine Mother, Herself. It is a deep mystery and a wonderful blessing that Divine Mother has consented to reside in this pattern. It is a great boon to see, own, or offer worship to a Sri Chakra of any kind, particularly one made of sphatika. When we offer worship to the Sri Chakra with love and devotion, the offering definitely reaches the feet of Sri Lalita Devi.

Every single line or angle in the Sri Chakra pattern is highly significant. The precise angles of the different triangles give us one-pointed focus towards the spiritual life.

The central bindu, or dot, is considered to be where Lalita Devi resides, and each triangle surrounding the bindu contains a different aspect of Lalita Devi's energy and power. The Sri Chakra also stands for the entire universe in its manifested state, which originates from the Divine Mother. Only Lalita Parameswari Herself fully understands the meaning of the Sri Chakra pattern and the profound impact and significance of its worship.

The Sri Chakra can be made as a two-dimensional drawing or etching in metal, or it can be formed into a three dimensional pyramid shape, with the central bindu as the peak. In its three-dimensional form, it is also known as a Meru Chakra, since 'meru' means 'mountain.' A Meru Chakra can be carved from many different materials, and each material will yield a slightly different effect. It is extremely powerful to have a Meru Chakra that is formed from gold, ruby or other precious stones, but of course this is not possible for most people. Meru Chakras that are made from clear quartz crystal are very powerful, and they are much easier to obtain than other kinds.

If one just views or touches a sphatika Sri Chakra, all the sins from many births will be destroyed. Performing worship to the Sri Chakra will be even more effective in washing away one's sins

One's noble and auspicious desires will be fulfilled if fragrant flowers are offered to the sphatika Sri Chakra. One can also offer kumkum or spoonfuls of milk. If 100,000 fragrant flowers are offered, Divine Mother is immensely pleased and will grant any wish.

A Sri Chakra made from sphatika is constantly attracting the most auspicious cosmic vibrations. These subtle cosmic rays are spontaneously transmitted to the person who touches, views or worships the sphatika Sri Chakra. Just as the sun casts its rays in all directions, the sphatika Sri Chakra will send these powerful cosmic rays out in all directions. This will purify and sanctify one's home tremendously. Solar energy is also attracted, which gives tremendous physical and mental benefits to the one who owns a sphatika Sri Chakra.

The sphatika Sri Chakra eradicates all of our defects, activates the intellect, and controls the wavering nature of the mind. The sphatika Sri Chakra also bestows knowledge and peace, as well as all siddhis, or auspicious divine powers. The cosmic rays emanating from the sphatika Sri Chakra protect one from the adverse planetary rays of Saturn, as well as Rahu and Ketu. These planets can sometimes cause difficulty or sorrow in one's life, but the sphatika Sri Chakra will protect one from every kind of negative energy. Ultimately, the sphatika Sri Chakra will even bestow spiritual liberation to the individual when it is worshipped with true love and devotion.

There are many different ways to worship the Sri Chakra, according to how much time one has. At the minimum, one should worship the Sri Chakra once a month on the full moon day. If one has more time, one can do worship every Friday, every Friday and Tuesday, or every day. There are some who offer worship three times a day, every day, but this is not possible for the vast majority of people.

If one is extremely strapped for time, one can simply chant the Devi Mantras nine times and offer a spoonful of milk with each mantra. Or, one can chant the Sri Suktam and offer milk with each sloka. One can also chant the 108 names of Lalita Devi while offering milk. One of the most auspicious ways to worship the Sri Chakra is to chant the Lalita Sahasranam, the thousand names of

Lalita Devi, while offering kumkum with each name. Some of the most auspicious items to offer include kumkum, turmeric powder, fragrant flowers or flower petals, or milk. If these are not available, one can add some turmeric powder to water and offer that.

The Significance of the Sphatika Lingam

Solar energy shines beautifully in the transparent sphatika Siva Lingam. Offering milk, water or vibhuti to the sphatika Lingam removes all curses and negative karma. When the Siva Panchakshari Mantra is offered 108 times, with milk or vibhuti, the darkest sins are destroyed.

If one chants the Siva Panchakshari Mantra 108 times with vibhuti, one obtains tremendous merit. If the vibhuti obtained from such worship is applied to the forehead, one's fate, which is written on the forehead by Lord Brahma, can be completely altered for the better. If one eats a pinch of that vibhuti, all poverty, sins and diseases can be destroyed.

If the Mrutyunjaya Mantra is chanted 12, 27, 54 or 108 times while offering milk, water or vibhuti, all illnesses can be cured. Accidents and other mishaps will also be prevented. Just by viewing the sphatika Lingam, sorrows and difficulties will be relieved.

Lord Siva is very fond of abhishekam. If the Siva Panchakshari Mantra is chanted 108 times while offering 108 spoonfuls of milk every Monday for twenty weeks, one's desire will be fulfilled.

Puja performed to a sphatika Lingam will enhance one's confidence and power. "Mantra siddhi," or the perfection of any particular mantra, can be more easily obtained when chanted before the sphatika Lingam with offerings.

The Benefits of Worshipping the Sphatika Ganesha

To remove any kind of obstacle or difficulty, one can offer milk to a sphatika Ganesha 108 times daily while chanting the mantra "Oṁ gam gaṇeśāya namaḥ." If one is able to obtain the holy "durva" grass, which is sacred to Lord Ganesha, one can offer it with the same mantra 108 times daily for forty days. This will fulfill any wish.

If one keeps a sphatika Ganesha in the home, one will be blessed with a duty-conscious mind, inspiration, and true discrimination during all works or tasks. Lord Ganesha will always be with one in subtle form as an adorable little boy. Wherever a sphatika Ganesha is present, murders, suicides and fire accidents will never occur. In His divine presence, all fear is destroyed.

If one views a sphatika Ganesha as soon as the eyes have opened after waking in the morning, without seeing anyone else first, all sins and hindrances will be destroyed.

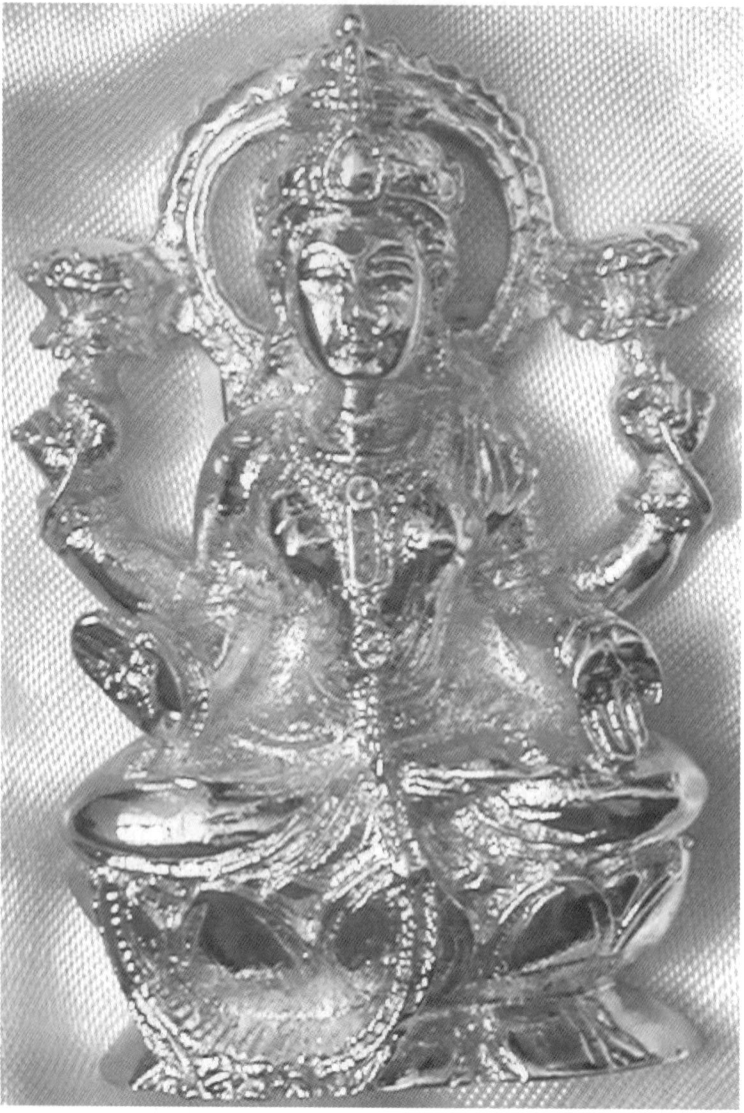

The Greatness of Worshipping Suvarna Lakshmi

Before this entire Creation existed, there was nothing but the self-luminous golden light of divine consciousness. The Divine Mother, whose original, true form is the golden energy of pure consciousness, created the entire universe out of Her divine radiance. Thus, in the Sri Suktam, Mother Lakshmi is described as having a complexion the color of molten gold, as being the very essence of gold, and as being surrounded with a beautiful golden halo. Having created the whole world, Mother Lakshmi pervades every inch of space with Her beautiful golden light. Everything in nature is suffused with Her golden light, but there are some materials that allow that light to shine forth to an exceptional degree.

On the Earth, the substance that retains the most powerful vibrational signature of Mother Lakshmi is the metal gold. There may be metals that are more rare, but no metal radiates the pure, spiritual vibration of Lakshmi Devi more so than gold. This is described in the Sri Suktam through the image of Lakshmi Devi wearing many beautiful and delicately wrought golden ornaments, like ear rings, necklaces, nose studs, bangles, and so on. These ornaments are not merely for decoration. Lakshmi Devi is setting an example for Her children, because when we wear golden ornaments, we stimulate the important nadis in our subtle body, such that our hearts are nourished with Divine Mother's energy and we become capable of expressing Her divine qualities in our lives.

Although the rishis have advised all people to wear at least one small piece of gold on the body, it is not necessary to wear gold as jewelry to benefit from its spiritual properties. It is extremely auspicious and spiritually uplifting to worship a murti that either contains gold or is gold-plated. Through the worship of a gold or gold-plated murti of Sri Maha Lakshmi Devi, all karma is destroyed, devotion is increased, and all forms of spiritual and material poverty are warded off. One's noble, spiritual wishes will be granted through worship of "Suvarna Lakshmi," or "Lakshmi of Golden Form."

A gold murti of Sri Maha Lakshmi is no different from Lakshmi Devi Herself, and it is a great opportunity to have Her presence in one's home in the form of a gold murti. Lakshmi Devi blesses Her children with affection, love and harmonious relations among all family members and friends. She brings peace and harmony to any home where She is lovingly worshipped, and She destroys all tendencies toward disturbance or commotion at the root. Those who have darshan, those who offer their salutations (pranam), and those who chant sacred hymns before Her will be blessed with inner peace, contentment and true devotion. Those who live in the house graced by the divine presence of Suvarna Lakshmi will never lack for the necessities of life, as they will always be in the care of Mother Lakshmi, who cannot bear to see Her children in pain or poverty.

It is extremely auspicious to chant the Sri Suktam before a gold murti of Lakshmi. The sacred vibrations in this Vedic hymn will activate the spiritual properties of the gold, and will attract the golden radiance of Lakshmi Devi to the chanter. If possible, it is even better to chant the Samputita Sri Suktam before Suvarna Lakshmi, as this chant contains the holy bijakshara "Srim." "Srim" is the seed sound for Lakshmi Devi Herself, and its repetition brings all auspicious blessings to the chanter, including radiant health, true devotion, contentment and material well-being.

Daily chanting of the Samputita Sri Suktam before a golden murti of Sri Lakshmi Devi is a wonderful general remedy for any kind of problem, whether material or spiritual. While chanting, it is very auspicious to offer fresh flowers of any variety. If the murti is solid gold, abhishekam can be performed with milk or turmeric water. If the murti is gold-plated, however, offering liquids may cause the gold coating to wear away. If flowers are not available, turmeric rice can be offered instead. Simply take uncooked white rice, like basmati rice, and mix it with turmeric and a small amount of ghee. The resulting golden-colored rice can be offered in small pinches before the lotus feet of Suvarna Lakshmi."

Please see the general puja guidelines below.

General Principles for Worship of Any Idol

Any container used to hold the item being offered should be completely unused before using it for puja. The spoon used to offer milk should also be completely unused and should not be used for other purposes once used for puja.

Puja items should not be made of iron or stainless steel. This metal attracts the energy of Saturn, which can create real difficulties for people. The best material for puja vessels is gold. It is not necessary for the entire vessel to be made of gold; it can also be gold-plated. Gold attracts the energy of the sun, and it is very beneficial to human health and vitality. It is also very easy to keep one's puja vessels shiny and clean if they are gold-plated, as gold does not become tarnished. The next best metal would be silver, and after that copper or brass. If these are not available, then any other material that is new and unused, like glass, plastic or paper, can be substituted.

There are two general ways to offer liquids to a mala or murti. In abhisekam, the milk or water is poured over the murti in a gentle, steady stream for the duration of the chanting. The other way is to use a spoon to pour just a spoonful of liquid onto the murti after completing each mantra or verse. Milk is very good to offer, and it is best if it is whole, organic milk. If milk is not available, water can be used for abhisekam or offering. It is good to add some turmeric to the water, especially for any Devi murti or Sri Chakra. The milk or water that has been offered to any murti can be drunk, as it will contain very positive spiritual energy. If it is not drunk, it should be poured over a tree or plant.

Anything that has been offered already should not be offered again. Kumkum or vibhuti that has been blessed and given by Amma should not be used for puja. When kumkum or vibhuti are being offered, remember to use the fourth finger and the thumb. Try not to let the index finger touch the offerings, as this finger contains the energy of the personal ego.

The most auspicious times for conducting puja are in the early morning around sunrise or in the twilight hours as the sun sets. It is ideal to perform puja after bathing and putting on fresh, clean clothes. White is a good color to wear for any puja. If desired, a small ghee lamp can be lit during the puja, although sesame oil can be substituted for ghee.

Ladies should avoid performing puja or touching any murtis during their menstrual period. It is best to do silent meditation during this time of rest and renewal.

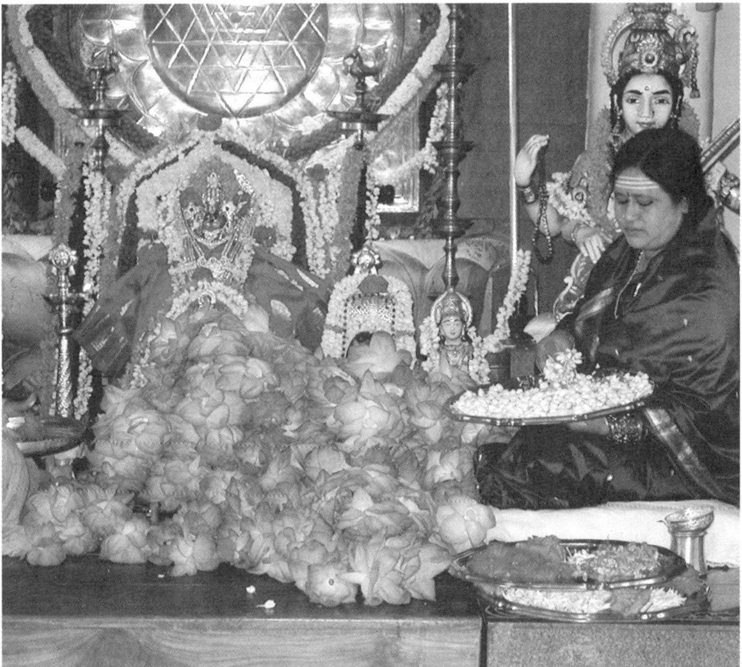

64

Mantra Summary

Mantra Summary

Ganesa Mantras

Oṁ gam gaṇeśāya namaḥ

Oṁ klīm gam gam gam mahāgaṇapataye namaḥ

Siva Panchakshari Mantra

Oṁ namaḥ śivāya

Siva Sakti Panchakshari Mantra

Oṁ hrīm namaḥ śivāya

Mrityunjaya Mantra

Oṁ trayambakam yajāmahe
sugandhim puṣṭi vardhanam
ūrvāru kamiva bandhanāt
mṛtyor mukṣīya māmṛtāt

Vishnu Mantra

Oṁ namo nārāyaṇāya

Devi Mantras

Oṁ śrī cakra vāsinyai namaḥ
Oṁ śrī lalitāmbikāyai namaḥ

Saraswati Mantra

Oṁ aim śrīm hrīm sarasvatī devyai namaḥ

Gayatri Mantra

Oṁ bhūrbhuvassuvaḥ
tat savitur vareṇyam
bhargo devasya dhīmahi
dhiyo yo naḥ pracodayāt
Oṁ āpo jyoti rasomṛtam
brahma bhūr bhuvas suvar oṁ

Rig Veda Lakshmi Mantra

Oṁ śrīm hrīm śrīm
kamale kamalālaye prasīda prasīda
śrīm hrīm śrīm oṁ
śrī mahālakṣmī devyai namaḥ

Saubhagya Lakshmi Mantra

Oṁ śrīm hrīm klīm em kamalavāsinyai svāhā